THIS JOURNAL BELONGS TO

From the Rising of the Sun

JOURNAL

BELLE GIFTS

Belle City Gifts
Savage, Minnesota, USA

Belle City Gifts is an imprint of BroadStreet Publishing Group LLC.
Broadstreetpublishing.com

From the Rising of the Sun JOURNAL
© 2017 by BroadStreet Publishing®

ISBN 978-1-4245-5591-8

Devotional entries by Michelle Winger.

All rights reserved. No part of this publication may be reproduced, distributed, or transmitted in any form or by any means, including photocopying, recording, or other electronic or mechanical methods, without the prior written permission of the publisher, except in the case of brief quotations embodied in critical reviews and certain other noncommercial uses permitted by copyright law.

Scripture quotations marked (NLT) are taken from the Holy Bible, New Living Translation, copyright © 1996, 2004, 2007. Used by permission of Tyndale House Publishers, Inc., Carol Stream, Illinois 60188. All rights reserved. Scripture quotations marked (NIV) are taken from the Holy Bible, New International Version®, NIV®. Copyright © 1973, 1978, 1984, 2011 by Biblica, Inc.™ Used by permission of Zondervan. All rights reserved worldwide. www.zondervan.com. The "NIV" and "New International Version" are trademarks registered in the United States Patent and Trademark Office by Biblica, Inc.™ Scripture quotations marked (NCV) are taken from the New Century Version®. Copyright © 2005 by Thomas Nelson. Used by permission. All rights reserved. Scripture quotations marked (NASB) are taken from the New American Standard Bible®, Copyright © 1960, 1962, 1963, 1968, 1971, 1972, 1973, 1975, 1977, 1995 by The Lockman Foundation. Used by permission. www.Lockman.org. Scripture quotations marked (NRSV) are taken from the New Revised Standard Version Bible, copyright 1989, Division of Christian Education of the National Council of the Churches of Christ in the United States of America. Used by permission. All rights reserved. Scripture quotations marked (ESV) are from the ESV® Bible (The Holy Bible, English Standard Version®), copyright © 2001 by Crossway, a publishing ministry of Good News Publishers. Used by permission. All rights reserved. Scripture quotations marked (TLB) are taken from The Living Bible copyright © 1971. Used by permission of Tyndale House Publishers, Inc., Carol Stream, Illinois 60188. All rights reserved. Scripture quotations marked (NKJV) are taken from the New King James Version®. Copyright © 1982 by Thomas Nelson. Used by permission. All rights reserved.

Design by Chris Garborg | garborgdesign.com
Edited by Michelle Winger | literallyprecise.com

Printed in China.

17 18 19 20 21 22 23   7 6 5 4 3 2 1

Give thanks to
the LORD,
for he is good!

His faithful love
endures forever.

PSALM 136:1 NLT

Continual Praise

*From the rising of the sun to its going down
The Lord's name is to be praised.*

Psalm 113:3 NKJV

What would it look like to be a woman who praises God from the time she awakens each morning until the time she falls asleep each night? Not only would we be pleasing God as we worship him constantly, but we would also effect an incredible change in our personal outlook.

As we go about our day, we can look for reasons to praise God. Out of an overflow of a heart of thankfulness, we will share God's goodness with those around us and give them a reason to praise his name as well.

Intentional, continual praise can only naturally result in intentional, continual joy. When we choose to look at each moment as a moment in which to be thankful and worshipful, then we will find in each moment beauty, joy, and satisfaction.

MY REFLECTIONS

From the end of the earth I call to you when my heart is faint.
Lead me to the rock that is higher than I.

PSALM 61:2 ESV

Your unfailing love is better than life itself;
how I praise you!

Psalm 63:3 NLT

You, O Lord, are good and forgiving,
abounding in steadfast love to all who call upon you.

Psalm 86:5 esv

There is no one holy like the LORD,
Indeed, there is no one besides You.

1 SAMUEL 2:2 NASB

Let the peace that Christ gives control your thinking,
because you were called together in one body to have peace. Always be thankful.

COLOSSIANS 3:15 NCV

All the ways of the Lord are loving and faithful
toward those who keep the demands of his covenant.

Psalm 25:10 niv

You are my hiding place and my shield;
I hope in your word.

PSALM 119:114 NCV

Give thanks to the Lord, for he is good;
his love endures forever.

1 CHRONICLES 16:34 NIV

The LORD your God is in your midst, a mighty one who will save;
he will rejoice over you with gladness.

ZEPHANIAH 3:17 ESV

Let us come boldly to the very throne of God and stay there
to receive his mercy and to find grace to help us in our times of need.

HEBREWS 4:16 TLB

Heavenly Rewards

Be patient, therefore, brothers, until the coming of the Lord. See how the farmer waits for the precious fruit of the earth, being patient about it, until it receives the early and the late rains.

James 5:7 esv

There is a prevalent message in today's culture that whispers sweet and appealing lies: rights to luxury and self-indulgence. You deserve it, Christian! God wants you to have it and to be happy. This whisper takes away the sweet truth of a God who rewards us, and injects the poisonous lie that that enjoyment must be immediate.

God wants to reward you. That is truth. He promises rewards to the faithful, and he keeps his promises. Those rewards are often not on this earth, and why would we want them to be? Earthly rewards are enjoyable, but they can be destroyed by moth and rust. Heaven's treasures are eternal.

To lean into the pull of God's kingdom instead of the tug of instant gratification, requires enduring patience. When you are tempted to give in to temporary satisfaction, remember the rewards that wait for you in heaven. Know that your loving Father is waiting to give you more than you could think to ask for. Let that spur you on in your works and actions, motivating you to live with a kingdom-driven mindset.

MY REFLECTIONS

The LORD is good; his steadfast love endures forever,
and his faithfulness to all generations.

PSALM 100:5 ESV

Always give yourselves fully to the work of the Lord,
because you know that your labor in the Lord is not in vain.

1 Corinthians 15:58 niv

I will praise you with an upright heart,
when I learn your righteous rules.

Psalm 119:7 esv

Be strong in the Lord and in his mighty power.

EPHESIANS 6:10 NIV

In all the work you are doing, work the best you can.
Work as if you were doing it for the Lord, not for people.

COLOSSIANS 3:23 NCV

You, God, are my God, earnestly I seek you;
I thirst for you, my whole being longs for you.

PSALM 63:1 NIV

Spread your protection over them,
that those who love your name may rejoice in you.

PSALM 5:11 NIV

"Rejoice in that day and leap for joy,
for surely your reward is great in heaven."

LUKE 6:23 NRSV

Guide me in your truth and teach me, for you are God my Savior,
and my hope is in you all day long.

PSALM 25:5 NIV

Let all that I am praise the LORD;
with my whole heart, I will praise his holy name.

PSALM 103:1 NLT

A Greater Wonder

*When I look at your heavens, the work of your fingers,
the moon and the stars, which you have set in place,
what is man that you are mindful of him,
and the son of man that you care for him?*

Psalm 8:3-4 esv

The God of all—the universe and everything in it—is the same God who gave his life to know us. The God who spoke the world into being is the same God who speaks quietly to our hearts. His love for us is as unsearchable as the heavens.

It's hard to believe that the Creator of the Universe is not only interested in us, but he is also invested in us. His love for us knows no limits or boundaries.

The greatness of our God is displayed majestically throughout his creation. When we look into the night sky at all the twinkling stars and the far-off planets, we realize almost instantly how small we are in his universe.

A greater wonder than the grandeur of God's capacity is his value for mankind. He is an incredible Creator who wants to be fully engaged with his creation. Let your mind ponder this throughout the day.

MY REFLECTIONS

Your beauty should come from within you—
the beauty of a gentle and quiet spirit that will never be destroyed.

1 PETER 3:4 NCV

This is the day the LORD has made.
We will rejoice and be glad in it.

PSALM 118:24 NLT

All heaven will praise your great wonders, LORD;
myriads of angels will praise you for your faithfulness.

PSALM 89:5 NLT

"The LORD rewards everyone for their righteousness and faithfulness."

1 SAMUEL 26:23 NIV

> He will keep in perfect peace
> all those who trust in him.
>
> ISAIAH 26:3 TLB

> Be kind and compassionate to one another,
> forgiving each other, just as in Christ God forgave you.
>
> EPHESIANS 4:32 NIV

God demonstrates His own love toward us,
in that while we were still sinners, Christ died for us.

ROMANS 5:8 NKJV

"I have told you these things so that you will be filled with my joy.
Yes, your joy will overflow!"

JOHN 15:11 NLT

Do not throw away your confidence; it will be richly rewarded.

Hebrews 10:35 NIV

Since we are receiving a Kingdom that is unshakable, let us be thankful and please God by worshiping him with holy fear and awe.

HEBREWS 12:28 NLT

Truly Special

*You are a chosen people, a royal priesthood,
a holy nation, God's special possession.*
1 Peter 2:9 NIV

We all want to believe that we are special. Most of us grow up being told that we are, and it feels good to believe it. But over time, we look around us and realize that, really, we are just like everyone else.

Sometimes doubt creeps in, making us second guess ourselves and damaging our self-confidence. Choose to believe today that God has called and chosen you for something truly special.

Long before you were even a wisp in your mother's womb, you were set aside and marked as important. You were chosen to be God's special possession, and that's pretty amazing.

Of all the people in the world, God has chosen you to do something only you can do. Ask him to show you what he has for you as you continue to walk in his wonderful light.

MY REFLECTIONS

> I wait for the Lord, my whole being waits,
> and in his word I put my hope.
>
> PSALM 130:5 NIV

Enter his gates with thanksgiving
and his courts with praise.

PSALM 100:4 NIV

> You make him most blessed forever;
> you make him glad with the joy of your presence.
>
> PSALM 21:6 ESV

You show me the path of life.
In your presence there is fullness of joy.

PSALM 16:11 NRSV

In perfect faithfulness you have done wonderful things,
things planned long ago.

Isaiah 25:1 niv

Everyone enjoys a fitting reply;
it is wonderful to say the right thing at the right time!

PROVERBS 15:23 NLT

Everyone will share the story of your wonderful goodness;
they will sing with joy about your righteousness.

Psalm 145:7 nlt

Let all that I am praise the LORD.
I will praise the LORD as long as I live.

PSALM 146:1 NLT

I will shout for joy and sing your praises,
for you have ransomed me.

PSALM 71:23 NLT

My whole being, praise the LORD
and do not forget all his kindnesses.

PSALM 103:2 NCV

In Sunshine and Storm

> When times are good, be happy;
> but when times are bad, consider this:
> God has made the one as well as the other.
> Therefore, no one can discover
> anything about their future.
>
> ECCLESIASTES 7:14 NIV

It's easy to feel happy on a sunny day, when all is well, the birds are singing, and life is going along swimmingly. But what happens when waters are rougher, bad news comes, or the days feel just plain hard?

God wants us to feel gladness when times are good. But he has made each and every day. We are called to rejoice in all of them whether good or bad.

Happiness is determined by our circumstances, but true joy comes when we can find the silver linings hidden in our darkest hours—when we can sing God's praises no matter what.

We don't know what the future holds for us here on earth, but we can find our delight in the knowledge that our eternity is set in the beauty of full relationship with our heavenly Father.

Make today a good day just because you know God loves you.

MY REFLECTIONS

"The Lord bless you, and keep you;
The Lord make His face shine on you."

Numbers 6:24 NASB

> "Lord, where do I put my hope?
> My only hope is in you."
>
> Psalm 39:7 NLT

Praise be to the God and Father of our Lord Jesus Christ,
the Father of compassion and the God of all comfort.

2 Corinthians 1:3 NIV

He alone is your God, the only one who is worthy of your praise,
the one who has done these mighty miracles that you have seen with your own eyes.

DEUTERONOMY 10:21 NLT

I long for Your salvation, O LORD,
And Your law is my delight.

PSALM 119:174 NASB

Our mouths were filled with laughter,
our tongues with songs of joy.

PSALM 126:2 NIV

Every good gift and every perfect gift is from above, coming down from the Father of lights with whom there is no variation or shadow due to change.

JAMES 1:17 ESV

No matter what happens, always be thankful,
for this is God's will for you who belong to Christ Jesus.

1 THESSALONIANS 5:18 TLB

Because you are my helper,
I sing for joy in the shadow of your wings.

PSALM 63:7 NLT

"Do not worry about tomorrow,
for tomorrow will worry about its own things."

Matthew 6:34 NKJV

Delightful

*The LORD takes delight in his people;
he crowns the humble with victory.*

PSALM 149:4 NIV

If ever there was something to lift your spirits and get you through the toughest of days, it's the knowledge that the Lord our God takes delight in you. He tells you so in his Word!

God takes pleasure in your very existence. Your heavenly Father created you to be in relationship with him, and he gets great joy out of it.

Revel in the knowledge of God's delight for all of today and into tomorrow. Embrace the fact that there is one who loves you and is truly captivated by you.

God loves spending time with you; he wants to get closer to you each day. Allow him to take you deeper! Dive in and experience his delight for yourself.

MY REFLECTIONS

Let everything alive give praises to the LORD!
You praise him! Hallelujah!

PSALM 150:6 TLB

God is King of all the earth,
so sing a song of praise to him.

Psalm 47:6 NCV

The Lord is compassionate and gracious,
slow to anger, abounding in love.

PSALM 103:8 NIV

You, O Lord, are a shield about me,
My glory, and the One who lifts my head.

Psalm 3:3 nasb

> Your lovingkindness, O Lord, extends to the heavens,
> Your faithfulness reaches to the skies.
>
> Psalm 36:5 NASB

"My grace is enough for you.
When you are weak, my power is made perfect in you."

2 CORINTHIANS 12:9 NCV

"Here I am! I stand at the door and knock. If anyone hears my voice and opens the door,
I will come in and eat with that person, and they with me."

Revelation 3:20 niv

"God resists the proud,
But gives grace to the humble."

JAMES 4:6 NKJV

Lord, teach me your ways,
and guide me to do what is right.

Psalm 27:11 NCV

There is surely a future hope for you,
and your hope will not be cut off.

PROVERBS 23:18 NIV

Look for Blessings

Oh, how great is Your goodness,
Which You have laid up for those who fear You,
Which you have prepared for those who trust in You,
In the presence of the sons of men!

PSALM 31:19 NKJV

Nothing moves us quicker out of our worldview, swirling around the god of self, than thankfulness to the true God. We can step outside of our world and into thoughts of him by examining the goodness he shows in the world, from big to small, A to Z. It is then that we see God touching every area of our lives.

God is not boxed up in the praise of our Sunday mornings or set down at the end of our Bible reading time. He is fluid and available, large and in motion, touching, moving, and breathing into the joints and ligaments of everyday life.

It creates an outworking of goodness in our lives when we acknowledge the goodness God has bestowed on us. We are moved to compassion when we thank him for moving in compassion toward us, and gratefulness stirs our hearts until it overflows.

Position yourself outside of your world to see God at work around you.

MY REFLECTIONS

The precepts of the Lord are right,
giving joy to the heart.

Psalm 19:8 niv

Be truly glad. There is wonderful joy ahead.
You love him even though you have never seen him.

1 Peter 1:6 NLT

Remember that you will receive your reward from the Lord,
which he promised to his people. You are serving the Lord Christ.

COLOSSIANS 3:24 NCV

Teach me your ways, O Lord, that I may live according to your truth!
Grant me purity of heart, so that I may honor you.

PSALM 86:11 NLT

"I am the resurrection and the life.
The one who believes in me will live, even though they die."

John 11:25 niv

The LORD will fulfill his purpose for me;
your steadfast love, O LORD, endures forever.

PSALM 138:8 ESV

Let us run with perseverance the race marked out for us,
fixing our eyes on Jesus.

HEBREWS 12:2 NIV

> I call to you, God, and you answer me.
> Listen to me now, and hear what I say.
>
> PSALM 17:6 NCV

Let my soul live and praise you, and let your rules help me.

Psalm 119:175 ESV

"Come to me, all of you who are weary and carry heavy burdens, and I will give you rest."

Matthew 11:28 NLT

Light of Love

How priceless is your unfailing love, O God!
People take refuge in the shadow of your wings.
Psalm 36:7 NIV

Whenever you start to doubt the love that God has for you, simply turn to his Word and be reminded of the truth. He picked you!

God wants a relationship with you, and he wants you to work with him to draw others into the light of his kingdom. Dive deep into your relationship with the Father. Out of a place of connection with God, you will draw others into his love.

Before we knew Jesus as our Savior, we lived in darkness. Now life is bright! Jesus is the lamp that illuminates the path ahead of us, directing us where to go and what to say and do.

Even in the darkness of the night, we are surrounded by his illuminating presence. Let's declare his praises together, and stay in the brilliance of his light.

MY REFLECTIONS